LEVEL 3

Written by: Nicola Schofield
Series Editor: Melanie Williams

T0345657

Pearson Education Limited
Edinburgh Gate, Harlow,
Essex CM20 2JE, England
and Associated Companies throughout the world.

ISBN: 978-1-4082-8835-1

This edition first published by Pearson Education Ltd 2014

11

Set in 17/21pt OT Fiendstar
Printed in Great Britain by Bell and Bain Ltd, Glasgow
SWTC/02/

Illustrations: Marek Jagucki

Published by Pearson Education Ltd

For a complete list of the titles available in the Pearson English Kids Readers series, please go to
www.pearsonenglishkidsreaders.com. Alternatively, write to your local Pearson Education office or to
Pearson English Readers Marketing Department, Pearson Education, Edinburgh Gate, Harlow, Essex CM202JE, England.

This is Peter and Pepper. They are going to summer camp with their friends. They are going on a spaceship ...

Their summer camp is on the moon!

This is Captain Cloud. He flies Galactic Airways to the moon every day. He looks out the window, and he sees three green aliens. They are jumping and shouting!

Suddenly, Captain Cloud cannot control the spaceship! The spaceship starts to make a terrible noise. They are flying much faster than before. It is very loud and noisy.

Peter and Pepper and their friends are afraid!

The spaceship stops. Where are they?

Where are we?
I don't like this.

I don't know. Don't be scared.

Peter and Pepper look out of the window.
They are surprised. This is not the moon!

Captain Cloud goes outside, and Peter and Pepper follow him. They see three green aliens. They look very different to the people on Earth. They have four eyes and four long arms.

Peter and Pepper do not know what to do. Peter is very afraid but Pepper is not. Their friends are also scared, but the aliens are friendly.

Hello. Welcome to Space Island! Don't be scared!

The aliens do not want to hurt the children. The aliens need their help. There is a big meteor, and it is coming to Space Island. The children have to save Space Island!

The aliens give Captain Cloud a map. The children have to follow the map and draw what they see in the spaces. Then they have to find the laser and put in the code.

Captain Cloud is happy.
He wants the children to help.
Peter and Pepper are excited!
They would like to help.

Peter and Pepper start their adventure. They walk for a long time. They come to a space village. They look at the map. What can they see?

Look! There's a big red rocket!

1 Space Village

3 Space Town

They look at the map. They have to go south. They arrive at a forest. The trees are round with blue and red leaves. It is different here. They see a blue elephant!

That's funny!

2 Forest

4 Astror

13

Peter and Pepper are enjoying their adventure. It is fun. Next, they arrive in Space Town. They see a big yellow building with young aliens inside. It is a school!

Can you see the teacher?

3 Space Town

Peter and Pepper move fast. They do not have much time. Pepper sees a building on the map. It is called Astronaut Café. They see people outside eating Astro cake. Peter and Pepper are also hungry.

Look at the cake!

Mmmmmm!

Peter and Pepper follow the map quickly and carefully. They swim across a river and climb a mountain. Suddenly they see a telescope on top of the mountain! They look through it. They can see Earth! It is beautiful!

_ _ _ _ U _

5 Telescope

But what happens now? What do they have to do? They see a picture of the laser on the map. They have to go to the laser now! The meteor is coming! They run fast!

LASER

CODE:

There it is!

Peter and Pepper are now at the laser.
They can see the meteor. It is coming
fast. Peter and Pepper have to be
quick. They have to find the
code for the laser!

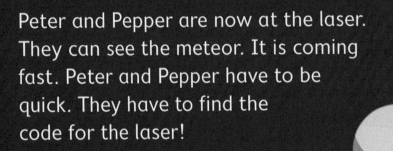

What's the code?

First letter please!

_ _ _ _ _ U _

Pepper looks at the pictures on the map.

Try this!

Last letter please!

R E S C U E

You are here X

LASER
CODE:
_ _ _ _ U _

① Space Village

② Forest

③ Telescope

④ Astronaut Café

⑤ Space Town

She reads the letters ... R for Rocket, E for Elephant, S for School, C for Cake and E for Earth! Peter puts the code into the computer.

The code is right! It works! A big light comes from the laser and hits the meteor! The meteor is falling fast. Peter and Pepper close their eyes and hold hands. They are rescuing Space Island!

Peter and Pepper open their eyes. Space Island is okay! There is no meteor now. Captain Cloud, the children, and the aliens are at the bottom of the mountain. They are happy and excited.

The aliens say thank you to the children. Captain Cloud, Peter, Pepper, and their friends fly away on the spaceship. They are going to their summer camp on the moon!

Activity page ❶

Before You Read

❶ Match the words and pictures.

1 aliens
2 rocket
3 telescope
4 map
5 laser
6 meteor

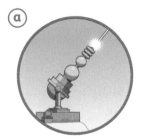  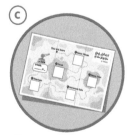

❷ Look at page 3. Who are Peter and Pepper?

Activity page ❷

After You Read

❶ Read and answer Yes (Y) or No (N).

a The children go to Space Island on a boat. ☐

b The aliens are not friendly. ☐

c Peter and Pepper help the aliens. ☐

d Peter and Pepper save Space Island. ☐

e The code for the laser is RESCUE. ☐

❷ Match the numbers on the map to the pictures a–e.

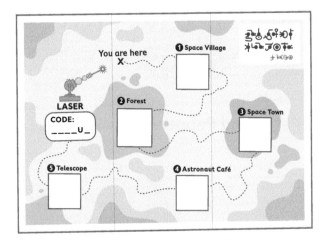

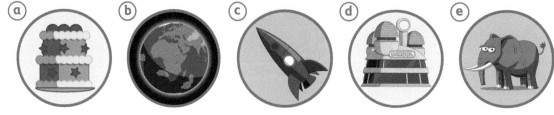

❸ Draw a picture of Peter and Pepper on their summer camp. Write what they are doing.